Your Dream Journal

Nighttime Dreaming

WITH STEPS, TIPS, & DEFINITIONS

Colleen Julia McShay De Silva

_____'S

DREAM JOURNAL

_____

date

Your Dream Journal by Colleen De Silva 2022

ISBN: 979-8-9865413-6-5

Cover photo by Graham Holtshausen on Unsplash

Author photo by Megan Marie - M.M. PHOTOGRAPHY

DEDICATION

I dedicate this journal to God, Jesus, and Holy Spirit who gave me the idea to write this journal, who gives me visions in the day and in the night, and who encourages me to be productive, present, and persevere. Without You, I would be sitting in a cafe only daydreaming instead of doing.

To my husband, Cory. Thank you for supporting me in all my aspirations and putting up with morning discussions of my nighttime dreams. You are my love.

To my son, Bryght, who has brought so much love into my heart. I cannot wait to hear about your nighttime dreams and see how God speaks to you.

To my family and friends whom I love very much. Thanks for letting me interpret your dreams. I dearly appreciate you all.

Gratefully, I dedicate this journal to all of you dreamers. Those of you who dream of impossible hopes and aspirations and those who dream in the night. I pray your dream-life increases and you have many God-given visions as the days come.

I am so blessed to be a part of your journey!

ENDORSEMENTS

"I absolutely love Colleen De Silva's *Your Dream Journal*. This is something I wish I would have written and published myself. She shows you how to practically record and journal your dreams and the meaning to many of the common symbols. This will radically impact you as you bring your night dreams into your daily life."

- Doug Addison
Author of *Understand Your Dreams Now*, Founder of InLight Connection and Spirit Connection Podcast, Blog, and Daily Prophetic Words

"I love how practical and powerful this journal is. Colleen makes it so easy for you to track, journal, and get revelation and understanding about your dreams. I personally had a dream coaching session with her that helped me understand what God was revealing to me in my dream. It is so good to see Colleen invest so much time and prayer into making this resource the most useful it can be. It speaks to who she is, and how much she cares about every person she ministers to. It will be so wonderful to hear how this journal blesses those who read and use it."

- Ray Leight
Author of *Identity Restoration* and *Finding a New Normal*, Co-Founder of Faith by Grace Ministries

"Colleen De Silva is a dreamer so her dream journal comes from experience not simply from theory. We were all designed by God to receive revelation and His hidden treasures often revealed at night in dreams. She also understands the importance of stewarding a dream. It is what we do with a dream that shows God He can trust us with more. *Your Dream Journal* is a tool to help us steward the dream as we take time with Holy Spirit to mine the treasures hidden within the dream. Let the treasure hunt begin!"

- Faith Blatchford
www.faithblatchford.com,
Author of *Winning the Battle for the Night: God's Plan for Sleep, Dreams and Revelation*

ENDORSEMENTS

"Stretch yourself awake from a great night's sleep and explore the endless treasure of dream interpretation with this self-discovery gem. *Your Dream Journal*, by Colleen Julia McShay De Silva, brings together simplicity, genius, and Holy Spirit inspiration. Remember what you used to forget, and unlock the wealth that flows while your spirit is active and your mind is at rest. Solomon speaks to these riches, and Colleen has given you a key to open the vault (Proverbs 3:24 and Proverbs 19:23). Don't miss another night. I know you'll love this journal as much as I do.

- Stephen K. De Silva
CPA (retired), author of *Money and the Prosperous Soul* and
founder of Prosperous Soul Ministries (a financial healing non-profit organization)

"Colleen is a gifted teacher who truly desires to help others hear God. This fun, compact, and anointed journal will hone your skills at dream interpretation. Each definition is profound, relevant, and, above all else, rooted in Scripture. Anyone interested in understanding their nighttime dreams should head out now and purchase it."

- Dawna De Silva
Co-founder of Bethel Sozo,
Author of *Sozo: Saved, Healed, and Delivered*, *Shifting Atmospheres*, and *Warring with Wisdom*

"There is a depth to Colleen's faith, and it is always evident to me how seriously she takes her walk with God. Colleen has been such a help to me personally. I was able to share my nighttime dreams with her and she asked meaningful questions that helped me hone in on the message and purpose of each dream. Taking it a step further, we were able to address any lies I was believing so that I could receive the truth and find healing from God. Colleen's gift set is gracefully powerful. She made the whole process feel like an adventure! She truly helped me at a pivotal time in my life, and I am so blessed that she continues to help others through Dreams Coaching."

-Kathryn Leight
Co-Founder of Faith by Grace Ministries

I encourage you
to steward your dreams
and see what possibilities
await you!

TABLE OF CONTENTS

INTRODUCTION

I decided to start journaling my dreams in 2011. Since then, I've had a dream, if not several dreams, almost every night. My nighttime dreams have also grown in details, frequency, and significance. The majority of my dreams encourage me, convict me, direct me, give me insight into the spirit realm and sometimes show me the future God has for me and others! I believe God loves to speak to us in the night while our body is resting and our spirits are awake. He wants to reveal His love, secrets, strategies, gifts, and hopes to us in the night, just as He does in the day.

I believe stewardship is extremely important if you want to see more dreams in the night and learn how to understand them better. This is one of the many ways God speaks to us and, honestly, it is probably one of my favorite ways to hear from Him because for me it is sometimes like playing detective with God!

I encourage you to steward your dreams and see what possibilities await you!

How To Use Your Dream Journal

1. **Read** the **STEPS, TIPS,** and **SAMPLE DREAMS** to get more understanding on how to journal your dreams.

2. **Use the left side of the journal pages to jot down your dream**. Jotting down your dreams can be writing only important things you remember, an outline, or every detail. It is up to you to determine how to best record your dreams.

3. **Fill in the date and title for each dream**. Filling this out is super helpful when you want to go back to a dream or remember it's significance.

4. **Pull from your dream** the **sections, objects, moments, people,** and **things that feel key** to interpreting your dream and write them down in the "Highlighted & Repeated" section on the right side of your journal pages.

5. **Use the DEFINITIONS to help with understanding key elements.** It's crucial to **read the "IMPORTANT" section first** as a reminder of how definitions can vary within different dreams depending on the context!

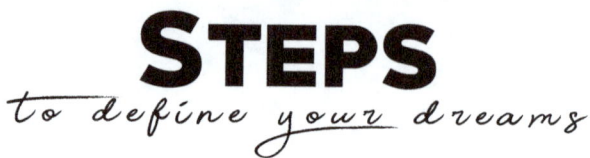

STEPS
to define your dreams

1. **Invite Holy Spirit** to join you and help you to remember.

2. **Record** your dream(s).

3. **Ask yourself** how the dream made you feel and write that down.

4. **Underline/highlight words, situations, actions, moments** that stood out to you.

5. **Underline/highlight** anything that **repeats** in the dream.

6. **Look up definitions** from the **Bible,** this **journal under "DEFINITIONS",** **dictionary, Biblical dream dictionaries** (Doug Addison's *Understand Your Dreams Now: Spiritual Dream Interpretation* and T*he Divinity Code to Understanding Your Dreams and Visions* by Adam F. Thompson & Adrian Beale are other great resources for definitions)

7. **Write** down the **theme/title**.

8. **Ask Holy Spirit any specific questions you have**. This is your time to spend with Jesus to find out more and understand your dream better.

9. **Write** down **what you hear from Holy Spirit** and **have fun.**

10. **Take any next steps,** such as **inner healing**, taking time to **pray for someone or something**, or **anything else you sense** about the dream interpretation.

TIPS
when exploring your dreams

1. **Seek Guidance from the Holy Spirit** — Dreams are invitations to interact with God and connect with His truths and purposes for your life.

2. **Think Positive** — See what the positive purpose or message is from the dream. Also, if you wake up feeling a negative feeling but it wasn't black and white, this may indicate a lie you are believing. If this is the case, God is showing you the lie and that your heart is ready to release it to Him to receive His truth.

3. **Record** — Record your dream regardless of whether or not you have time to interpret it. Even if it's just a few words that will spark the memory of certain moments from your dream for when you do have time to look back and interpret it.

4. **Birds-Eye View** — Take a step back from the dream. See it from a birds-eye view instead of a magnifying glass. This will help you to see the dream as a whole instead of nit-picking it.

5. **Title** — Come up with a fun title for your dream. This can help you see from a birds-eye view.

6. **Your Definitions** — Think about how you relate to different objects, places, people, and things instead of solely relying on various book definitions. Do the definitions produce hope, peace, or correlate with the theme? If it's a conviction from God, it may cause you a short period of grief but it always moves you closer to God, Jesus, and Holy Spirit.

TIPS
when exploring your dreams

(CONTINUED)

7. **Bible** — Look up key elements in the back of your Bible under "Concordance."

8. **Nightmares into Positives** — Turn your nightmares into strategy and intercession dreams, or simply hand them to Jesus and ask Him where He was when you had the nightmare. Let Him lavish you with His love.

9. **Metaphors** — Dreams are usually metaphorical and not literal.

10. **To Tell or Not Tell** — Wait and ask Holy Spirit who the dream is for. Then don't assume you are supposed to tell that person immediately. Instead, ask Holy Spirit if you are to tell the person about the dream or not. A lot of times, we are meant to simply pray for them. Negative dreams are typically intercession dreams for that person(s) or place(s).

11. **Definitions May Differ for Others** — When helping others interpret their dreams, remember that their definitions of people, places, and things may be different from yours and keep it positive.

12. **Play on Words** — A tissue in a dream may be pointing out an "issue", "T(issue)". Another example, the name Cody could be referring to "Co-De... pendency." This is why seeking guidance from Holy Spirit is most important (Tip #1).

DEFINITIONS
in alphabetical order

IMPORTANT (READ FIRST):

These definitions give just a few possible interpretations for each object, place, person, and thing. Remember to look at your dream as a whole. Match the definition with the context of your dream. You may need to think about what an object does or what it means to you. For example, a can opener opens canned foods. So one definition could be that you need a tool or have just found a tool to get the spiritual food you need.

Another possibility... if you don't own a can opener and have been praying for one (in the dream or in real life), the dream could be signifying that God is about to bless you with an answered prayer or a desire you have. To go further, if the food you opened is food you love, then God could be telling you that this blessing (can opener) is a tool to bring you into a dream fulfilled.

An alternative interpretation... if the food is old and/or the only food left, then I would explore the possibility that God is showing you that you believe the lie that the tools God gives you are not good or good enough. That they lead to a poverty lifestyle. It could also be the lie that He doesn't want to give you the desires of your heart. The rest of the dream would help you see what the truth is and/or lead you into an inner healing time with God.

As you can see, these definitions cannot stand alone! They have to align with the theme of your dream and make sense as a whole. When figuring out what specific things in your dreams mean, really ask yourself what those objects did, how they made you feel, and what they reminded you of. Does a person or object from your dream remind you of a Bible verse? A movie? A parent? A friend? A lot of times we search online, but, in reality, God is speaking to us directly and He knows us! So take a step back and ask yourself, "What did the dream mean to me?" If you're still stuck, ask Father God to show you and give you understanding. Remember to invite Holy Spirit into this entire process.

DEFINITIONS
in alphabetical order
(CONTINUED)

With that in mind, there may be definitions that are not written here or explained in other resources. Ask the Holy Spirit which definitions relate to your dream.

Enjoy exploring your dreams!

✷✷✷✷

AIRPLANE: move of God (large passenger airplane - holds many people and takes them to the same destination), higher calling (travels high in the sky), transition to calling (travels from one destination to another), going one place to another

ALLIGATOR: deception (camouflaged animal of the water), demonic spirit (Isaiah 27:1)

BABY: gift from God (Matthew 1:21), miracle (Isaiah 7:14), God's promise (Galatians 4:23-28), Holy Spirit (Galatians 4:4-6), blessing (Deuteronomy 7:13)

BACKPACK/BAG: the sin you carry (Job 14:17), burden (Matthew 11:29-30), stewardship (Matthew 25:14-30), survival, comfort from worldly possessions (Mark 6:8)

BALCONY: prophetic view/higher perspective (seeing from above), clarity or lack thereof

BAREFOOT: walking on Holy ground/in God's presence (Exodus 3:5), walking without peace/faith/Holy Spirit/grace (Isaiah 11:15), striving/walking in flesh (Ezekiel 16:10)

BASEMENT: the foundation of an aspect of your life/an issue/a lie/a habit (basements are foundations of a house), resting place (Jonah 1:5)

BATHROOM: repentance/cleansing/washing of sins (John 13:5-10), healing (John 9:11), old issue (old bathroom), childhood issue (childhood bathroom)

BED: rest, intimacy, marriage (Hebrews 13:4), agreement/partnership - sharing the bed with someone or something (Isaiah 57:8)

BEDROOM: private space (2 Kings 11:2), union/intimacy (2 Samuel 11:2-4)

BICYCLE: striving or striving towards destiny (riding a bicycle takes leg work/own strength), recreation/play (when it's a loved sport/hobby/recreation)

BIRTH(ING): beginning of something new/exciting/joyous (John 16:20-21), a gift from God, birthing a gift/calling/career/new responsibilities from God, gift from interceding (1 Samuel 1:10-18)

BOAT: life's journey (Genesis 7:1-24), Holy Spirit transportation, sail boat - moving in the Spirit (wind can represent Spirit) (John 3:8), speed boat - fun and fast transportation by the Holy Spirit

BOOK : Godly wisdom (Joshua 1:8), worldly wisdom, accessible wisdom, guidance (Hebrews 10:7), instruction/law (Exodus 24:3-7), knowledge, the wisdom you carry (carrying books), remembrance/history/memories/record (Esther 2:23, 6:1-2) (Psalm 56:8)

BOY(S): young(er) generation(s) (Genesis 17:9-14), heir/legacy/inheritance (Genesis 18:16-19) (Genesis 21:1-7), promise (Genesis 17:15-21) (Genesis 21:1-7), miracle (Genesis 18:9-15) (Genesis 21:1-7), boy(s), check the name definition of his/their name(s) if you know the boy(s)

BUILDING(S): Individual (temple for the Holy Spirit) (1 Corinthians 6:19-20), building oneself or another up (positive [1 Corinthians 6:19-20] or negative [Genesis 11:5-8])

BUNNY (RABBIT): multiplication, prosperity, fertility (Genesis 1:22), unclean (Leviticus 11:6)

BUS(ES): group of people going in the same direction/same calling, aspect of life headed towards destiny (Acts 1:8), transitioning from one place to another

BUTTERFLY: transformation (2 Corinthians 3:18), identity, coming into your identity (from caterpillar to butterfly) (Romans 6:6), glorified through rest, dying from old self (Romans 12:2)

CAR: takes you to your destiny, aspect of life, self,
old/vintage car - old self/business/ministry (Matthew 9:17)

CAT: independent spirit (cats are known for their independence), companion (positive or negative), the occult/witchcraft (black cat in culture is often associated with witches/fear/superstition)

CHILD(REN): peacemaker(s) (Matthew 5:9), followers/believers of God/Jesus/Holy Spirit (Matthew 7:11), humbled individual(s) (Matthew 11:25) (Matthew 18:3), follower(s) of evil/satan/the devil (1 John 3:10)

CITY: people (Genesis 4:17), specific place, the world (Genesis 11:4), called to this city or what it represents (Matthew 2:23)

CLOSET: quiet/private place (Matthew 6:6)

CLOTHING: God's covering/protection (Genesis 3:21), ashamed/embarrassed (Genesis 3:7), favor (Genesis 37:3), grief/grieving (tearing one's clothing) (Genesis 37:34)

COLLEGE: a season of training for what's next (Luke 2:41-52), spiritual training (1 Timothy 4:8), a season of preparation for new opportunities/a new season/etc., a season of testing (spiritual/character)

COLORS:

BLACK - darkness, death (Job 30:30), gloom (Job 3:5), void of life (Genesis 1:2-3), hidden, night, God rules the night/dark/darkness (Psalm 139:11-12)

BLUE - revelation, heaven(s)(ly) (Exodus 36:8)

BROWN - earth (color of dirt), dirty/sin (John 13:5-10), healing (John 9:6)

GOLD - holy/refinement (Job 23:10), finances/wealth/money/rich/power (Genesis 44:8), valuable, anointing/favor (Zechariah 4:11-14) (Ezekiel 16:13), glory, blessed (Genesis 24:35), religious glory (Revelation 17:4), idolatry (Daniel 3:1)

GRAY - lukewarm/mixed/indifferent/neutral (gray is black and white combined)

GREEN - new, alive/life (Genesis 9:3), earth (color of grass) (Genesis 1:30), growth/prosperity (Isaiah 53:2), anointing (olive green) (Deuteronomy 33:24), unclean/sin (Leviticus 13:47-49)

PINK - redemption in purity (red [blood of Christ] & white [purity] mixed) (Hebrews 13:12), childhood innocence/young/youthful (1 Samuel 17:42), girl/feminine (common color associated with girls), flesh/fleshly/unclean (Leviticus 13:42)

PURPLE - royalty (Judges 8:26), authority (Daniel 5:7), kingship (John 19:2), righteousness (Exodus 28:15)

RED - blood/redeemed/purified (Hebrews 13:12), covering/protection (Exodus 36:19), new covenant (Hebrews 12:24), anger/wrath of God/curse (Exodus 7:19), compassion (1 Peter 1:2), stop (culturally stop signs are red)

SILVER - refined/purified (Psalm 66:10), pure words/God's words (Psalm 12:6), second (second place medal), rich (Genesis 13:2), payment/money/payment (Genesis 24:53; 45:22), atonement/reconciliation (Exodus 30:15–16)

VIOLET - royalty (Esther 8:15)

WHITE - pure/purified/cleaned/righteous/righteousness/holiness (Isaiah 1:18), purity/worthy/innocence (Revelation 3:4-5), Holy Spirit, spirit, glory/light (Matthew 17:2), ready for harvest (John 4:35), conquerer/conquering (Revelation 6:2), angel (John 20:12), false prophecy (from the phrase "whitewashed" - to cover up uncleanliness/wrongdoing/error/unpleasant situations) (Ezekiel 13:10-11), light (Matthew 17:2)

YELLOW - warning/caution/fear (cultural - yield signs are yellow), happy/bright (associated with cultural view on the color of the sun), unclean (Leviticus 13:30-36)

COMPUTER: connection (used to connect with people around the world), networking (culturally used to network), in the head (intellect - I.T. [information technology]), programmed (learning/downloading through computers) (Romans 12:2)

CROWD: busyness/busy (Mark 2:4), a specific generation (if it is the same age group), collective of people (literal meaning - notice what type of people are in the crowd), isolation (if in the midst of a crowd unnoticed), cloud of witnesses (Hebrews 12:1), public (Nehemiah 8:3), following worldly/fleshly people - with the world (Exodus 23:2), not following the crowd (if going the opposite direction of crowd this could be positive as in not conformed by the world [Exodus 23:2] or negative - depends on what the crowd represents), distressed/downcast (Matthew 9:36)

DARK(NESS): choosing a life without welcoming God (Job 3:4-6), hidden/unknown (cannot see far in front of you) (Daniel 2:22) (1 Corinthians 4:5)

DEATH: justice (Exodus 21:12), new life (Romans 6:4)

DINING ROOM: communion (Jesus broke bread at the table) (Matthew 26:26-29), community/gathering place (cultural for people to gather to eat), place for wisdom to be received (food as wisdom) (John 4:34) (Matthew 4:4)

DOG: companion (positive or negative), best friend ("a man's best friend" cultural phrase), demon (if attacks or deceives) (2 Kings 9:36), greedy/unsatisfied persons (Isaiah 56:11), evil workers/enemy (Philippians 3:2)

DOOR(S): opportunity, opened door to a spirit (positive [Psalm 24:7] or negative [Genesis 4:7]) or to Jesus (Revelation 3:20), protection (2 Kings 4:4) (2 Kings 6:32) (Isaiah 26:20), mouth (Psalm 141:3)

DOVE: Holy Spirit (Matthew 3:16, Mark 1:10), messenger (Genesis 8:8-12)

DRIVER'S LICENSE: identity (identification card), citizenship (shows where you live)

EAST: the promised land (Numbers 32:19), sun or son rising (the sun rises in the east), God's glory (Ezekial 43:1-5), waiting on God (Jonah 4:5)

FIRE: God (a consuming fire) (Hebrews 12:29), Holy Spirit baptism (Acts 2:3), judgement (Genesis 19:24), Hell/torture (eternal fire) (Matthew 25:41), Heaven consuming an offering/sacrifice (2 Chronicles 7:1), refinement (Matthew 3:10)

FISH: people (Matthew 4:19), money/finances/financial blessing (Matthew 17:27), provision (Luke 5:6) (Luke 9:16-17), mass people in the spirit (swarms of fish in the water) (Matthew 4:19)

FLOWERS: clothed by God (Matthew 6:28-30), temporary (Isaiah 40:8), provision, beauty, divine revelation/honor (almond flower) (Exodus 37:17-22)

FLYING: high calling in the spirit (Isaiah 40:31), high perspective (seeing from a raised level), free in the spiritual realm/hopes in the Lord (Isaiah 40:31), an object flying - gone/comes and goes/not lasting (Proverbs 23:5), safe from attacks (Ephesians 2:4-6), above/Heaven's perspective (Ephesians 2:4-6).

FOOD: Jesus (bread) (John 6:35), celebration (Ecclesiastes 9:7), provision (Exodus 16:2), wisdom/God's will (John 4:34, Matthew 4:4), God's love (Psalm 136:25), worship (1 Corinthians 10:31)

FUNERAL: new season/change (Joshua 1:1-6), old habit dying, death to old self (Romans 6:4), honoring the past or a person (2 Chronicles 21:19) (Jeremiah 34:5), letting something/someone/past go

GASOLINE: fuel for the soul/body/spirit (gasoline is used to fuel a vehicle to keep it moving)

GAS STATION: a place for refueling for your soul/body/spirit (gasoline is used to fuel a vehicle to keep it moving/operating), a place to be filled with the Holy Spirit (Acts 2:4)

GIRL: young(er) generation(s) (Genesis 17:9-14), hope/promise/miracle (Matthew 9:18-25), young church (Ephesians 5:23)

GOLF: engulf (play-on-words "in golf"), course of life (golf course) (Proverbs 27:17) (Proverbs 16:9)

GREEN CARD: adopted by God, on your way for citizenship or authority, permanent resident (gives permission to permanently live in North America), identity/identification (used for identifying people)

HELICOPTER: higher perspective (seeing from the sky, building tops, etc.), rescuing/intercession (police helicopter)

HOUSE: destiny, aspect of life (Matthew 7:24), person (Matthew 24:43), old house - old issue or old lie, a place of provision and shelter (Genesis 19:3) (Genesis 24:31), specific rooms indicate other possible definitions

HURRICANE: move of the Spirit (positive (John 3:8) or a negative spirit), refinement, disaster coming or warning (a call to intercede) (Acts 27:1-26)

ISLAND: isolation, vacation, alone time, rest, temporary rest/safety (Acts 27:25-26, 28:1-2)

KEY: resource for opening a door (1 Chronicles 9:27), a gift from God (Matthew 16:19), fear of the Lord (Isaiah 33:6), revelation, tool - either spiritual (Matthew 16:19) or physical (Judges 3:25), wisdom (Luke 11:52), authority (Isaiah 22:21-22)

KITCHEN: preparation for wisdom/to do God's will (a place to prepare food - food as wisdom/God's will [John 4:34] [Matthew 4:4]), storing wisdom (food as wisdom)

LAMB: Christ (lamb of God) (John 1:29), young Christian and follower of Jesus (John 21:15), innocence (1 Peter 1:19), sacrifice (Genesis 22:8), offering (Leviticus 3:7)

LOCK: self-protection (a locked door to protect yourself from people, Jesus, God, Holy Spirit, disappointment, etc.) (John 20:19-23), needing a key (gift/wisdom/tool) for an opportunity/to move forward/for freedom (Galatians 3:22), the law (Galatians 3:23)

MAN: image of God (Genesis 1:27), old self (old man), can represent a specific type of man or person (depends on the man's actions, name meaning, career, etc.), fear of man (can be seen as being afraid of the person or trying to people-please) (Proverbs 29:25) (Isaiah 51:7), wisdom or man's wisdom (older man) (Leviticus 19:32) (Job 12:12) (Job 32:6)

MAP: direction (Matthew 2:13) (Proverbs 16:9) (Proverbs 3:5-6), atmosphere, a call to intercede for a location shown

LEAVES: a season ending (leaves falling - represents fall is ending and winter is coming), saying goodbye to a situation or place (death of the leaves), play-on-words (she/he/they/it leaves), spiritually dead (Isaiah 1:30), wrath of God/justice (Jeremiah 8:13)

LEPROSY (SKIN SORES): unclean (Matthew 8:2-3), partnership with pride (2 Chronicles 26:19), affliction (2 Chronicles 26:20)

LION: God (lion to Judah) (Hosea 5:14), Jesus (Lion of Judah) (Revelation 5:5), devouring spirit, enemy (1 Peter 5:8)

LIVING ROOM: relaxing place, community/fellowship (a place where family and friends gather)

NAKED(NESS): vulnerability, shame (Genesis 3:7-10) (Revelation 3:18), childlikeness/innocence (Genesis 2:25)

NUMBERS:

ONE - single, the beginning (Genesis 1:1), creation (Genesis 1:1-5)

TWO - double, double blessing, covenant/unity/marriage (Ephesians 5:31)

THREE - trinity (2 Corinthians 13:14), resurrection/death to resurrection (Ephesians 5:31), miracle/time for miracles (John 2:1-12), bearing fruit or seed (Genesis 1:11-13)

FOUR - coming into promise (Genesis 15:16), creativity, world impact (Genesis 1:14-19), seasons (Genesis 1:14)

FIVE - grace/favor/redemption (Benjamin was given five times as much food to show Joseph's grace, favor, and redemption for his familly [Genesis 43:17-34]), five-fold ministry, life (first day of living/moving creatures [Genesis 1:20-23])

SIX - human (creation of man and woman on sixth day [Genesis 1:27-28]), fruitful/multiply (Genesis 1:28), authority (Gensis 1:28), striving/strife (Exodus 16:5) (Exodus 20:9) (Exodus 23:10), flesh (creation of flesh/humans on sixth day [Genesis 1:27-28])

SEVEN - completion/finished (Genesis 2:1-2), rest (Genesis 2:3), holy/perfect (Genesis 2:3)

EIGHT - new beginnings (the 8th day after God rested was the first day that all existed together [Matthew 28:1])

NINE - gift (a baby is born in nine months), fruitfulness (nine fruits of the Spirit)

TEN - commandments (Exodus 34:28), law (Joshua 8:31-32), rules/guidelines/guidance (Deuteronomy 5:1)

ELEVEN - transition (Deuteronomy 1:1-8), refinement (Judas sinned and then died, then there were eleven disciples [Mark 14:10] [Matthew 27:3-5] [Matthew 28:16])

OIL: anointing (Zechariah 4:11-14), consecration (Luke 7:36-50)

OLIVE(S): anointing (Zechariah 4:11-14)

OWL: night creature/spirit (Isaiah 34:15), one which resides in the wastelands/desert/desolate places (Psalm 102:6), unclean creature/spirit (Leviticus 11:13-18), alone/loner/abandoned (Psalm 102:3-6), nocturnal/awake in the night

PASSPORT: permit to travel outside of authority, new authority, new territory, new access in the physical or spiritual realm

PERSON(S): name definitions, who they are to you, may represent a generation or type of people, may be a play-on-words (Aaron is errand and Cody is codependency [co-dy-pendency])

PHONE: communication, reaching out to someone or God/Jesus/Holy Spirit, connection or lack of connection (having trouble getting a hold of/reaching someone)

PLACE(S): direction (Matthew 2:13), atmosphere, a call to intercede for location shown

PREGNANCY: awaiting a promise to be fulfilled/expectancy of God's promises (Genesis 18:12-14) (Luke 1:8-17), miracle (Luke 1:26-30) (Matthew 1:1-25), favored/entrusted with a gift (Luke 1:26-33), no longer barren (Luke 1:8-17) (Genesis 18:12-14, 21:1-7), grace (Genesis 21:1-7), giving birth to mischief and lies (if the person represents or has partnered with wickedness or if baby comes out wicked) (Psalm 7:14-16)

RABBIT (BUNNY): multiplication/prosperity/fertility (known to produce a large number of offspring very quickly), unclean (Leviticus 11:6)

RAINBOW: God's promise(s) to us/promises (Genesis 9:11-17), God (Revelation 10:1-7)

RING: promise/commitment/covenant (engagement/wedding ring), power/authority (Genesis 41:37-42), specific gems can indicate more definitions, a beautiful woman without discretion (gold ring in a pig's snout) (Proverbs 11:22)

SCHOOL: a season of training for what's next (Luke 2:41-52), spiritual training (1 Timothy 4:8), a season of preparation for new opportunities/a new season/etc. (a place that prepares you for life/career/etc.), a season of testing (indicated by taking a test) (spiritual/character)

SHARK: evil devourer in the spirit realm (water represents the Spirit and a shark devours), spiritual attack (shark attack), a call to intercede for a specific group of people (body of water can be body of the Holy Spirit/Jesus/God)

SHIPS: slow progress towards destiny (type of slower transportation), aspect of life headed towards or away from God's plan (Acts 27:9-22), journey (Psalm 107:23-24), ministry (Psalm 107:23-24), a person(s) (James 3:4), faith (1 Timothy 1:19)

SHOE(S): your walk (covered [with shoes] or not covered [without shoes]), peace/following God (Isaiah 11:11-15) (Proverbs 16:9), a lack of peace (shoe-less), on holy ground (taking shoes off0 Exodus 3:5), inheritance/ownership (Ruth 4:1-12) (Deuteronomy 25:5-10), exchange/transaction/redeem (when a shoe is given [Ruth 4:7-8])

SNAKE: demonic attack that does not affect you (if the snake bites and does not affect you) (Acts 28:3-6) (Mark 14:16-18), demonic attack that affects you (if the snake bites and it affects you in the dream) (Genesis 49:17), sign of God's power/Himself (Exodus 7:8-13), deception (Genesis 3:1-7)

SPACECRAFT: transportation/transition from one place to another, an aspect of your life that is bringing you to see from God's point-of-view, heavenly or spiritual perspective (reaches high and allows you to see from far above)

SPIDER: demon/oppressor/evil/liar (Isaiah 59:1-13) (Job 8:14), religious spirit (white spider [false righteousness - white represents righteousness/purity]), death or the occult spirit (black widow [venomous and known to eat male after copulation]), the flesh or deception (black spider [black represents flesh/deception]), caution for demonic attack or stronghold/spirit of fear (yellow spider (yellow represents caution/warning/fear), supernatural hero (Spiderman)

STAGE: influence (a place where you are to reach more people at once), platform, seen (people watch those on a stage), to be heard and seen/has a message to share (Matthew 5:1), in the spotlight, high calling, play-on-words "stages" of life (Numbers 33:2)

TEETH: pride (broken teeth) (Job 4:10), loss of pride (if broken teeth fall out) (Job 4:10), wisdom (wisdom teeth), false wisdom (loose/falling out/missing wisdom teeth), treacherous person (bad tooth) (Proverbs 25:19)

TELEVISION: play-on-words "tell a vision," insight, influence (reaches a multitude of differnt people in different places)

TOMB(S): spiritually dead/not followers of Jesus (Matthew 23:27)

TORNADO: spirit (Holy Spirit/God/positive [Numbers 11:31] or not God/negative [1 Kings 19:11]), attack of destruction (Kings 19:11), wind of change/shifting (if the tornado switches directions or shifts things), turning, judgment (Exodus 10:13), doubt (tossed by the wind) (James 1:6)

TRAIN: a flying train can be a huge move of God (in the wind flying [in the Spirit] and carrying lots of people), vehicle to your calling (transports people to a destination), in transition, on track (train is on track moving in forward direction), play-on-words to "train" or "training" (Proverbs 22:6) or a "train" on a dress/coat/robe (Isaiah 6:1)

TREE: can indicate a person's character (Matthew 12:33), strength/wisdom (deep-rooted tree) (Colossians 2:6-7), a dream fulfilled (Proverbs 13:12), you or others/people/person (Matthew 7:15-20), sacrifice (Jesus hung on a tree [Acts 5:30, 10:39, 13:29])

TRUCK: aspect of life (see context of dream), transitioning to destiny/calling

UNICORN: strength/power (Numbers 24:8), imagination (is known as a nonexistent animal on Earth today), supernatural/thinking outside the box/unique (culture)

UNIVERSITY: a season of training for what's next (Luke 2:41-52), spiritual training (1 Timothy 4:8), a season of preparation for new opportunities/a new season/etc., a season of testing (spiritual/character)

VOLCANO: eruption of the Holy Spirit (Matthew 3:11), regional refinement (Matthew 3:10), eruptions of what the volcano represents, person who erupts/explodes/bursts in rage (culture sometimes calls this volcanic anger), sudden destruction, destruction/judgment (Isaiah 30:30-31)

WALL: boundary (positive [protecting you from evil] [Nehemiah 2:7-8]) or negative [when it keeps disease/evil/lies in] [Leviticus 14:36-42]), self-protection, security, safety/barrier (Jeremiah 5:22), something keeping you from your calling or God's gift (Hebrews 11:30)

WALLET: finances/provision (holds money), identity (holds ID cards/driver's license), prosperity, a source of identity or provision (holds money, credit/debit cards, ID cards/driver's license)

WATCH: God's timing (Habakkuk 2:3) (Galatians 4:4) (Peter 5:6) (Psalm 37:7), flesh's timing (1 Samuel 13:8-14), specific time on watch can refer to Bible verses or the season (look up specific number meanings) (Ecclesiastes 3:1), play-on-words "watch" (Matthew 26:41), seen and protected (Psalm 61:7)

WATER: Holy Spirit (living water/river) (Revelation 7:17) (John 7:38)(John 4:10), man-made/man's spirit (man-made lake), unclean spirit (dirty water), stale in the spirit (stagnant water), be still in the Spirit (in still water) (Psalm 46:10), movement of the Spirit (rushing), constant Spirit (waves are constant), big moves of God or a spiritual attack (big waves)

WIDOW: free from law (Romans 7:1-6)

WIND: Holy Spirit (John 3:8), doubt (tossed by the wind) (James 1:6), demonic attack (Job 1:13-19)

WINDOW: prophecy (positive or negative) (1 Kings 13:14-17), revelation (comes from Heaven) (Isaiah 24:18), perspective (positive or negative) (Proverbs 7:6-7), eyes ("eyes are windows to your soul" concept) (Matthew 6:22-24), a portal to Heaven (Genesis 7:11, 8:2) (Malachi 3:10), a way to escape (Joshua 2:14)

WOMAN: caretaker (1 Timothy 5:16), concerned about the things of the Lord (a single woman) (1 Corinthians 7:34), concerned about the world (a married woman) (1 Corinthians 7:34), church (Ephesians 5:22-24), glory of man (1 Corinthians 11:7)

ZOMBIES: spiritually dead people/not followers of Jesus (zombies are not alive) (Matthew 8:22) (Matthew 22:32), people who feed on intellect (zombies eat brains) (Genesis 3:1-13)

Sample Dream

DREAM <u>10/17/2021</u> : <u>Praise God to Win Warefare</u>
          date   theme or title

I was outside, it was nighttime. I was with (a group of people). We maybe just flew or something. And (just arrived) somewhere that felt like (a desert town) or something of this sort.

I was under attack. I heard a voice say to me (I thought was Holy Spirit but I wasn't sure - normally I am 100% sure in a dream it is or isn't). "If you don't do something then the (Hyperion) (felt like in the dream that it was the most dangerous evil spirit of existence or the name of a mythical creature (which I found out is)).

Then I saw a liger (lion & tiger mixed) coming towards me. So I repented for opening doors to any sin, asked forgiveness and forgave others. I did and said everything and every tool I have ever learned to make sure I was pure. Then, I felt someone

Group: people going in the same direction or going through a similar warefare, season, promise, etc. Or generation.

(Desert): preparation place before promised land. Acts 7:30

(Hyperion) is a Titan from Greek Mythology. He was solely just a father of three celestial deities (sun/moon, Dawn) (Makes me think of a false father) He also was represented a sun with is sun.

22

behind me holding me. I thought it was Jesus at first and even felt this person squeeze me tightly on and off. At first, I felt protected but then each time this person behind me squeezed. He would squeeze tighter and tighter! At times I couldn't breathe and it hurt. So I turned around to see who was actually behind me instead of assuming (I thought this can't be Jesus). The face was wide-eyed and felt creepy. I said, "GET OFF OF ME!" I broke free I said, "YOU'RE NOT JESUS! GET OFF OF ME!"

I jumped back and saw everything coming after me to attack me and I was overwhelmed. I said to myself, calmly "Okay, nothing I am doing is working. What has God told me that works?" Then, I remembered praising Him/singing praise to Him. So despite the overwhelming attacks

(right margin notes:)

This squeeze was tangible! I also recognized it was numbing me & causing me to freeze. NOT FROM GOD.

As soon as I recognized and commanded with authority. The demon had to release me!

My eyes saw what the enemy was doing around me. But it wasn't important that I didn't let it affect my peace.

23

around me, I calmed myself down and just began to focus on Him. I suddenly felt Heaven on Earth. All the attacks around me were black and white and I realized they were like movies. They could not affect me or touch me anymore. As if all attacks were holograms!

It seemed like because I was so focused on the attacks that I was being deceived that they were affecting me but in reality they were not affecting me at all!

Then, suddenly, as I continued to sing praise to God. I saw several others doing the same. We were all coming together! I thought to myself, in the dream, "They figured it out too!"

"Heaven was showering the Earth like stars rushing down like rain."

Holograms! "black & white" I grasp that means plain & simple / clean / clarity cleanly defined

☆ This made me feel like this is a word and a new strategy for God's children. How to win in spiritual attack & warefare

24

DREAM <u>10/17/2024</u> : <u>Praise God to Win Warfare</u>
date theme or title

Interpretation:

The interpretation felt very clear for this one! God was giving me insight and strategy on how to lift deception and win Warfare.

He showed me that when we turn our focus to Him, deception is lifted. We will see clearly. That the attacks are simply a facade! That even focusing on ourselves and perfecting ourselves will not lift us from deception or lies. That the best solution is praising Him. For me, sing to Him gets my focus on Him, His power, His love, His truths, His fatherhood, and on Heaven's perspective.

I believe this is a new season and important strategy for now!

That the attack of the enemy can only affect us when we give power to them. They are holograms & of film. Just how virtual realities and films affect us — the energy was the same to play with our emotions to & cause us to sin.

25

I'm excited for you
to be transformed by God
through your nighttime dreams!

Have fun!

DREAM

_____ : _____

date   *theme or title*

DREAM

_____ date

: _____ theme or title

_____

_____

_____

_____

_____

_____

_____

_____

_____

_____

_____

_____

_____

_____

_____

_____

_____

_____

_____

_____

DREAM

:

theme or title

Highlighted & Repeated

DREAM

_____ : _____

_____

_____

_____

_____

_____

_____

_____

_____

_____

_____

_____

_____

_____

_____

_____

_____

_____

_____

DREAM _____ : _____

Highlighted & Repeated

DREAM _____ : _____
date   *theme or title*

_____
_____
_____
_____
_____
_____
_____
_____
_____
_____
_____
_____
_____
_____
_____
_____
_____
_____
_____
_____
_____
_____
_____

DREAM

_____ : _____
theme or title

Highlighted & Repeated

DREAM

_____ : _____
date   theme or title

Highlighted & Repeated

DREAM _____ : _____

Highlighted & Repeated

_____

_____

_____

_____

_____

_____

_____

_____

_____

_____

_____

_____

_____

_____

_____

_____

_____

_____

DREAM

_____ : _____

date *theme or title*

DREAM

_____ : _____
date   *theme or title*

DREAM

_____ : _____
date   *theme or title*

Highlighted & Repeated

38

DREAM

_____ : _____
date   *theme or title*

DREAM

_____ : _____

Highlighted & Repeated

DREAM

_____ : _____
date   theme or title

DREAM

_____ :_____

Highlighted & Repeated

DREAM

_____ : _____
date   theme or title

DREAM

_____ : _____
date   theme or title

Highlighted & Repeated

DREAM

Highlighted & Repeated

DREAM

_____ : _____
date   *theme or title*

Highlighted & Repeated

_____

_____

_____

_____

_____

_____

_____

_____

_____

_____

_____

_____

_____

_____

_____

_____

_____

_____

_____

_____

_____

DREAM

_____ : _____
date   *theme or title*

_____

_____

_____

_____

_____

_____

_____

_____

_____

_____

_____

_____

_____

_____

_____

_____

_____

_____

_____

_____

47

DREAM

Highlighted & Repeated

DREAM

_____ : _____
date   *theme or title*

DREAM

date   *theme or title*

Highlighted & Repeated

DREAM

_____ : _____
date   theme or title

DREAM

_____ : _____
date   theme or title

_____

_____

_____

_____

_____

_____

_____

_____

_____

_____

_____

_____

_____

_____

_____

_____

_____

_____

DREAM

_____ : _____
date   *theme or title*

_____

_____

_____

_____

_____

_____

_____

_____

_____

_____

_____

_____

_____

_____

_____

_____

_____

_____

_____

DREAM

_____ date : _____ theme or title

_____

_____

_____

_____

_____

_____

_____

_____

_____

_____

_____

_____

_____

_____

_____

_____

_____

_____

_____

DREAM

_____ : _____
date   *theme or title*

DREAM

:

Highlighted & Repeated

DREAM

_____ : _____
date   theme or title

Highlighted & Repeated

DREAM

_____ : _____
date   *theme or title*

Highlighted & Repeated

DREAM

_____ : _____
date   theme or title

DREAM _____ : _____
date *theme or title*

Highlighted & Repeated

DREAM

Highlighted & Repeated

DREAM _____ : _____
theme or title

Highlighted & Repeated

_____

_____

_____

_____

_____

_____

_____

_____

_____

_____

_____

_____

_____

_____

_____

_____

_____

_____

_____

DREAM _____ : _____

Highlighted & Repeated

DREAM

_____ : _____

date *theme or title*

Highlighted & Repeated

DREAM

_____ : _____
date   *theme or title*

Highlighted & Repeated

DREAM

_____ date _____ : _____ theme or title _____

DREAM

:

Highlighted & Repeated

DREAM

_____ : _____

date　　　　　　　　　　　　*theme or title*

Highlighted & Repeated

_____

_____

_____

_____

_____

_____

_____

_____

_____

_____

_____

_____

_____

_____

_____

_____

_____

_____

_____

DREAM

_____ : _____
date *theme or title*

_____

_____

_____

_____

_____

_____

_____

_____

_____

_____

_____

_____

_____

_____

_____

_____

_____

DREAM

_____ : _____
date   *theme or title*

DREAM

date : theme or title

DREAM

_____ : _____
date   *theme or title*

DREAM

_____ : _____
date   theme or title

_____

_____

_____

_____

_____

_____

_____

_____

_____

_____

_____

_____

_____

_____

_____

_____

_____

DREAM

date : _theme or title_

Highlighted & Repeated

DREAM _____ : _____
date   *theme or title*

Highlighted & Repeated

DREAM

_____ : _____
date   *theme or title*

_____

_____

_____

_____

_____

_____

_____

_____

_____

_____

_____

_____

_____

_____

_____

_____

_____

_____

DREAM

_____ :_____
date   theme or title

_____

_____

_____

_____

_____

_____

_____

_____

_____

_____

_____

_____

_____

_____

_____

_____

DREAM

_____ : _____

date *theme or title*

Highlighted & Repeated

DREAM

Highlighted & Repeated

DREAM

_____ : _____

date   *theme or title*

DREAM

_____ : _____
date   *theme or title*

_____

_____

_____

_____

_____

_____

_____

_____

_____

_____

_____

_____

_____

_____

_____

_____

_____

DREAM _____ : _____
date   *theme or title*

Highlighted & Repeated

DREAM

_____ : _____
date   theme or title

_____

_____

_____

_____

_____

_____

_____

_____

_____

_____

_____

_____

_____

_____

_____

_____

_____

_____

DREAM

_____ : _____

date   *theme or title*

Highlighted & Repeated

God loves to speak to us in the night
while our body is resting
and our spirits are awake!

ABOUT THE AUTHOR

Colleen Julia McShay De Silva

Colleen Julia McShay De Silva is a Dreams Coach, author, award-winning actor, and award-winning filmmaker. She is a guest author in Ray Leight's *Maturing Into Yourself* book, having written chapter twenty-three "Dreaming Again". Colleen has a Bachelor of Arts degree in English Literature from Indiana University and is a graduate of Bethel's School of Supernatural Ministry in Redding, CA.

She resides with her husband, Cory, and her son, Bryght, in Los Angeles, CA where she pursues both her creative dreams and coaching practice. When she first started stewarding her nighttime dreams, she never imagined the impact it would have for herself and others. Colleen loves pursuing a dream-fulfilled life with perseverance and God's purpose in mind. She hopes to help others do the same.

Colleen's other interests include going to the beach and traveling across the U.S. to visit her family. Colleen adores singing and writing songs with her husband. She is working on other books, screenplays, and journals.

HOW TO FOLLOW HER

INSTAGRAM: @colleenjdesilva
FACEBOOK: Colleen J. De Silva
YOUTUBE: Colleen De Silva
WEBSITE: www.colleendesilva.com

OTHER RESOURCE RECOMMENDATIONS

For combating nightmares and setting yourself up for a good night's sleep:
Winning the Battle for the Night and ***Good Night and Sweet Dreams***
by Faith Blatchford

For more information on understanding your dreams:
Understand Your Dreams Now: Spiritual Dream Interpretation
by Doug Addison

For more definitions, sample dreams, and information on dream interpretation:
The Divinity Code to Understanding Your Dreams and Visions
by Adam F. Thompson & Adrian Beele

For more definitions and information on dream interpretation:
Dream Elements: An Alternative Dream Dictionary
by John E. Thomas

For practical steps to partner with God in changing bad dreams
into a strategy that defeats the plans of the enemy:
Dream Changer
by Beth Chiles

www.ingramcontent.com/pod-product-compliance
Lightning Source LLC
Chambersburg PA
CBHW082110120626
46553CB00011B/3623